No Passing Zone

Poems

Donna Reis

DEERBROOK EDITIONS

PUBLISHED BY
Deerbrook Editions
P.O. Box 542
Cumberland ME 04021
207.829.5038
www.deerbrookeditions.com

FIRST EDITION
© 2012 by Donna Reis
all rights reserved
ISBN: 978-0-9828100-5-7

Book Design by Jeffrey Haste
Cover photo: Gary Firstenberg

For my mother and father

and

for Tom

Contents

III

No Passing Zone

I

And who's to say I didn't cross
just because I used the bridge in its witnessing,
to let the water stay the water
and the incongruities of the moon to chart
that joining I was certain of.
                                   —Tess Gallagher

Still Life

I want to go back to the woods
where snow heated
my back and blanketed my legs
as I waited to be found.

To the woods where a tree stood
in that opalescent sea
where I drifted between life and death.

I want to feel that stillness
only lovers and the dying feel
before they go beyond.

I want snow
to light on my face
the way it did as I lay
that night like a fallen tree,
an ailing wolf.

I want to be alone
with the steam that rose
from my legs as blood
pooled into snow.

I want to remember
how I tried to hold on
as I floated
in and out.

I want to go back
to the woods where pain
lifted me with paced breaths
as I became the ground
and the night
and the snow.

Green Stairs

Somewhere between the time
I finish painting our staircase and dinner,
you notice all the other chores
I began and left
compelled to work my way down
to where the bottom step meets the floor.
I drink in the new mossy green,
much better than the scuffed Colonial blue
worn for two decades,
but you're tired and only see the blistering pain
between my shoulder blades, the glassy look
in my eyes, and wonder why
I take on so much.
You find the stripped bed, sorted laundry
heaped on the floor, dirty pots
piled in the sink, knowing you'll have to finish
what I started,
while I savor the rich luster of
freshly painted risers against pine treads
and imagine how they'll rise
before us as we plod
up to bed
for the next twenty years.

Secrets

It's getting harder and harder to talk
to people because I have a secret.
The truth is my secret has a secret,
which is that it never really happened,
yet it's so pitiable, adultery and
murder pale beside it—my long shame
of not having a secret
big enough to keep.

Sleeping with the Carpenter

The carpenter is downstairs
spreading Spackle over Sheetrock.
I'm stalling my nap
until he leaves.

He and I have been together
in the house all day: me in my office,
he in the kitchen.
Floorboards, joists, and beams

lie quietly between us.
I don't mind him here,
because it means we're closer
to a finished kitchen.

He will leave soon
without saying goodbye,
his only thought, getting home
to his wife and children.

Yet, I still wait to hear his truck
crush gravel as it turns
out of the driveway
before falling asleep.

Everything You Need to Know about Ghosts

First let go of the idea
they're enlightened.
All those times
you held your tongue,
certain someone would
get his in the afterlife
were vain. Truth be known,
some specters are as nasty
after death as before.
Second, try not to fall
for their stories of how
they chose not to cross
the amber river
because of some dangling
injustice, some unresolved
mystery. Don't be swayed
by the old excuse
of not knowing they're dead.
Try not to be impressed
by their translucent togas
glowing like heavenly-lit scrim,
this outfit is merely to give weight
to a last goodbye at three in the morning,
an unearthly warning.
Remember they never use doorways,
yet they always take the stairs.
For extra drama, they curl like smoke
or swoop behind you as a disembodied head,
releasing an effluvious odor,
a maniacal laugh. Don't count on them
for anything so practical as finding
your keys, because they are undoubtedly
the ones who hid them.

Texas

We haul suitcases off the carousel,
and lug them, along with a headache
I picked up somewhere over Ohio,
into the sun, climb in back of the family
Cordoba and head past pawn shop
after porn shop down to Jack's
funeral parlor. Parched prairie grass
flutters along highways like mourners.
A crow whines from a steeple-top
and I want to stop the car
see if I can talk to him.
I want to tell him about Pop,
how he sang and tap danced
in vaudeville when he was eight,
how he said his Hail Marys
on daily drives to and from the market,
how he thanked God every day
that I'd married his son.

The crow wheels around the steeple
where I'm certain Pop is up
in that belfry's dim, narrow room,
kneeling before a narrow bed under Jesus'
sacred heart because someone
once told me a bell ringer
is the closest person to God.
I hear him singing psalms,
his voice swirls
up the winding stairs
around the clapper and climbs
toward his beloved saints.
I listen to his gentle vespers
as his suit keeps time on its hanger,
the necklace of rosary beads
ticking against the car window.

Fireflies

Every June out on Jessup Road
my husband wakes me in the middle
of the night leading me in my nightie
and slippers down the drive to witness
the meadow teeming with millions
of tiny lights. Better than any meteor
shower, these small engines render
us too innocent to capture them in jars,
or clasped hands to watch the spaces
between our fingers flash—
or worse, smash their radiance
into our skin,
that fleeting blaze of holiness,
beautiful and damned.

Needle's Eye

To Stephen, my acupuncturist, and George,
the hit-and-run driver who veered off the road
in his Ford LTD.

As you implant the first round
of needles into my feet, I tell you
my nightmares,
my dread of dark streets,
of headlights' screech, of icy metal
of grills and hoods.
You remember everything
I can't.
Memories swirl from scars
as my blood bursts from your palms.
You think back to the doctor who foretold
my death during the night,
the prayer groups, nurses who called
me "Tiger" or "Humpty Dumpty"; recall
your retort to the doctors who requested X-rays,
"Which volume?";
remember lifting my splintered spine
as you slid film beneath me
juggling
tubes, traction and tar, ballooned
thighs; recall how I squelched pain
as I do today,
the thirty-second
anniversary of the drunken
driver who hit me and left me
by the side of the road,
where I found you
and you found me,
again.

My back hurts.
Take the ache
into your
hands.

Perseverance

Pursed lips, never veer astray, stay
the course, barely breath, wait
for help. Float corridors,
morphine-high, foraging for food.
I see it's meat-loaf day in the cafeteria.
But you haven't left your bed
in four months. Wait like a poet
at the mailbox. I can tell
this is my bed by the NPO sign taped
to the headboard and the drip, drip
dripping of the IV. I wait
like a swallow to fly back
to Capistrano. I saw my nurse
crying in the phone booth.
That's not possible. You say
I survived because God has something
special in mind for me—perhaps
that's more than I can bear.

Night

Sister, night is so vast our boats so small.
—Li-Young Lee

There is always a reason not to sleep.
Eyelashes net the sky. Nails pop
from walls like typos. My mother's birthday
I'd rather not acknowledge, but do.
Rooms recite her last letter,

but I can't bring myself to listen.
I place it in my hope chest next
to my baptismal gown hoping
the victory lock will shut her in
or out. I slip through the screen door

and climb the hill to my dog's grave,
he and I watch the stars from the fallen
black locust. A bear and her cub
disappear into tall grass so quickly
I'm not sure they exist.

Six Degrees

The painter and I are hardly acquainted
except that I was the one who asked for stripes

and he is a friend of my husband's ex-girlfriend Jill
who used to be best friends with Debbie

whose house I'm about to drive to
to pick up my co-op order. Debbie was the first

girlfriend of my ex-boyfriend Bill
whom I lived with in Manhattan.

Bill's best friend was Dean
who married Debbie after Dean's mother

had Bill arrested and placed in rehab.
Then Bill dated Betsy who was also

in rehab and was Debbie's best friend
before Jill. Betsy's sister, Subee,

was Dean's first girlfriend
and Dean's brother Jim's first girlfriend

and Bill's girlfriend after me.
Dean's brother Jim's best friend

was another Jim whom I lived with
before Bill, long before

I met my husband
whose name is also Jim

whom I met at Dean and Debbie's
while he was dating Jill, who knows

our painter, Bill,
who's upstairs fretting

about time lost painting stripes.

View from the Playground

Across the fence
two junked cars aim out of the pond.
Ellen and I are certain they're
sinking in quicksand.
We gauge water levels
rising from fender to hood
ornaments, admire their gangster
roundness, their peeling blue
and green paint.

We decide they're getaway cars
with money strapped in sodden
valises alongside bodies in trunks.
In a chase, they screeched past their turn,
spraying glass bullets as they tumbled
like gray fedoras into brown water—
interiors filled with moonlight
as mobsters were caught in handcuffs.

We could blow away a whole day,
Ellen and I, side by side on our swings
trying to reach over the fence
with our feet as our stories rose
like heat waves from cars'
rusting roofs. We'd walk home
the adventure of the heist
cooling with our sunburned faces.
I still dream myself behind the wheel,
police hot on our tail
as we shoot
toward the Jersey line.

Centrifugal Force

Where I grew up
there were cars that doubled
as boats, cute little things
with propellers. We'd see
them driving down Jersey
Avenue with seaweed and
water streaming from their
fenders. There were planes
that landed on the lake.
They'd bob up and down
while we swam, then lift
like Pegasus.
There was Goose's Ford
Falcon; we'd pile in, drive
to the middle of the ice,
slam on the brakes and spin,
and spin and spin. And let's
not forget the *"Deep Six"*,
the patio boat we all chipped
in for. We'd down six-packs,
jump in the water, pee, climb
back on and do it again.
It sank within three weeks.

Please Bear with Me

while I bare my soul. Don't
be such a bear—I don't expect
you to respond, in fact, I couldn't bear
it if you did. Just so you know, I can bare
much more and have. I've bared myself
in the backs of cars and under
lifeboats on crowded beaches. Could I bear
even a brush with death? I have,
in fact, I've borne four. So don't fret
if your silence leaves me naked.
I can bear it, even grin.

II

. . . And look! my last, or
next-to-last, of three loved houses went.
The art of losing isn't hard to master.

—Elizabeth Bishop

Plumbing and Psychosis

As I lie on the stiff, papered table
my doctor asks, How is your kitchen
coming along? Horribly, I reply
our plumber never came back
to install the sink. He twists his face,
suggests I start Prozac.

I wonder how pills will summon
the plumber. Had I added that none
of the appliances or cabinetry
were installed,
because we don't have a floor,
would he have prescribed lithium?

And if I'd trudged in a year earlier
after bailing sewage
from our living room, would he have blurted
Mellaril? And what about when the house
started to pitch and we discovered
its main support beam had rotted?

Surely that was worthy of Haldol
or Thorazine. Suddenly it all makes sense—
contractors, plumbers and electricians
don't return phone calls, because
they're blurred in a druggy haze
of indifference bouncing from

month to month like astronauts.
My doctor thumps my stomach, asking,
And what about your bathroom?

Rage

is a woman
knowing every ridge
of a man's body
only to have her affection
of two decades
splayed on a couch,
not like a beached whale,
for those whales are forlorn
and repentant, but like a stain
left by the slow decay
of everything that matters.

Sempronia

For Mary Ann Lamb (1764 – 1847)

It was the kitchen that undid me,
all that slicing and chopping,
stabbed by Mother's criticisms
and the metallic glare of those knives.

To cut loose I had to plunge
one through Mother's heart,
so I could write, write, write.
The asylum was better than cooking,

better than being hanged.
And it wasn't long before my brother
Charles got me out. Out of air
I cleaved poems, children's stories

and the first protest against
women's unpaid labour, yet only
my brother's name could appear
on my half of *Tales from Shakespeare*.

Still he and I grew famous for
our Wednesday night soirees.
Shelley attended a few, and Coleridge,
the Wordsworths and every writer

passing through London for a night or two.
They found me graceful and gay
not at all insane, they didn't know
after they left the kitchen rattled

toward me, its knives hissing,
Mary, Mary, be a little lamb . . .

Dorothy at Grasmere

For Dorothy Wordsworth (1771 – 1855)
We talk over past days, we do not sigh for any
pleasures beyond our humble habitation
'the central point of all our joy.' —D. W.

At dawn I pad through the cottage
careful not to wake William,
start the kitchen fire,
heat up yesterday's broth for breakfast
and place it perfectly on the table
beside a plate of bread and butter.
Having already eaten, I jot
down my brother's stanzas,
so he can savor the orchard from the window
or finish poem "To a Butterfly."
How he struggles
to put my vision to verse.
No matter, I will bake pies,
bread and seed cakes to ease his fretting,
then harvest my scarlet beans
to serve with ham and milk for dinner.
While he naps I will walk
and walk, perhaps to Rydal
to see if there is a letter from Coleridge,
then home for tea and this morning's
cakes. Before supper I will show
William my anemones, sweet peas
and journals to rally his muse.
Then I will serve a nice piece of cookery
from boiled gizzards and mutton
or maybe a partridge with a hard-boiled
egg and a rhubarb tart.

Protecting My Husband from Peaches

To keep you from gritting your teeth
and shuddering in the grocery store,
I handle the peaches.
I mine golden orbs, heft their plumpness,
pressing their flesh for ripeness.
How can you do that, you ask.
Home in our kitchen, I spoon several
into boiling water, turning them over
and over until I can peel the skins
that repel you. I show you the sunny spheres
like a mother who opens her child's closet
to prove there's no monster. Then I puree
them with buttermilk and apple juice,
toss in a teaspoon of spice and honey,
a dash of good luck and rose petal for joy.
You sip the chilled nectar and bless me
for charming nettled fruit
into savory soup.

Going for Coffee after an Al-Anon Meeting

To get through each day,
I kill my husband, Sandy says.
I imagine him driving home
through the night silence
of a blizzard, wipers clicking
back and forth clogging with snow.
Blinded, he crashes through a guard rail
plummeting 200 feet into a ravine.
Then there is the funeral. I go
all out looking fantastic,
dabbing my eyes and pouting
in my new black dress.
I already have it hanging
in the closet and I'm dieting
for the fatal occasion, she adds,
while twisting her foot round
like a cat flicking her tail.
Lynette confesses, I've been praying
for lightning to strike.
My husband is on our tin roof
replacing flashing around the chimney
when a thunderbolt rockets him
into our neighbors' hedges,
his last sip of Jack Daniel's dribbling
down his chin. And, yes,
I too have the black dress.
I got it at Bergdorf's.
How can he complain about the $1,200
price tag when it's for his funeral?
Cheryl admits, I actually almost killed
my husband once—I was so furious
I knocked him out with the vacuum hose.
If you try this,
you should use a steel hose—

those plastic ones
won't do a goddamned thing.

Beliefs

Where do storms go when the stars come out,
when their human litter is scattered about . . . ?
—Tom Miller

The bridge snaps into the drive
snug as a train track, stone
scallops of wall on either side.
Depending on your belief,
it seems to have evolved or
been created one hundred
years ago. I have faith
it will hold, my husband
of one month does not.
Certain it will cave in,
he climbs underneath daily
to gauge the stream's defiance.
I try to convince him that storms
that destroy only come once
a century, but he's on to my
tender white lies. He predicts
oil trucks crashing through
girders and spilling into Satterly
Creek to anyone who'll listen,
while I envision rippling down-
river entwined on a rubber raft,
an open picnic basket on the bank.

Vicodin

Suicide as an idea seeps into your lungs like nerve gas.

—Mary Karr

I always keep a Vicodin
handy because anything could
happen: I could lose another home,
be the casualty of another
hit-and-run driver,
or catch a narrow glimpse
of myself. I finger the pill's
oval hardness like a worry stone.
A couple in Berlin kept
two cyanide tablets hidden.
When the Nazis stormed
their apartment, they were
gone, lying in bed,
holding hands. I reach
in my pocket
for a narrow escape.

Missing Boy

Grafton our bloodhound is summoned
to find the Lewis boy.

He snuffles a dirty sock
and drags us to Bristol Bridge.

Steel girders cut through water
where it never freezes,

where black ice moans
cracking under our feet.

Parents search pewter-colored
mountains as a psychic crawls

on her hands and knees
around the boy's house.

She says over and over,
He's in a cold place, very cold.

Evidence

I have an aversion to cell phones,
especially yours—
that black box leaking
forbidden desires,
past liaisons, a song learned
just for you. I know
because I listened
as I dropped or sunk
to the bottom
to find the missing,
a mechanical flaw.
Hang up, I yell, but can't
help myself, haven't been able
for years. One too many
lost marriages, too many glasses
of wine, too many departures.
And now what?
Am I the desperate hijacker
who combusts into flames,
or the blanket that smothers
and smolders?

Two Rooms Left

to decorate. Only
then can I leave this house,

after I paint the bedroom
apricot, buy red curtains,

even though we're broke,
because I need this house,

which has eroded our home
with each crumbling wall.

I have stopped talking
to our dead dog, so I can leave

his grave behind, stopped
wishing for things I can't have.

Still all I have is a house.

Cowboys

You're devouring stories about cowboys.
You're getting twinges that
wring the breath out of you.
You almost pass out
at the sight of Marlboro billboards.
A man in boots asks you
where the copier machine is
and you have to restrain yourself
from going down on him.
You want to be his open prairie,
want to feel his spurs in your sides.
You feel like you're cheating
on your husband, feel you should
wish he were home more often.

Forgotten

She barely remembers being married
although it meandered for twenty years.
Stone lodged in her heart, hardening
even as she worked at something
as mundane as lining pantry shelves.
She'd stop ten minutes before
he came home so she wouldn't
have to hear how she could have
done it better. All those times he halted
his hand at the tip of her nose,
saying, I'm not finished speaking.
She'd wait, and wait, and wait…
until she forgot
what she was going to say.

No Passing Zone

How is it I've returned
to this road?
It was snowing then
as it is now.
It is dusk.
Stone walls that once
split my forehead tumble
over the path where Hansel
and Gretel trailed bread.
The witch warned, Beware
of cars that pass on the right.
Keep off the shoulder,
as I was milled to dust
that now lights on your doorsill
like silent snow.

III

it's far too late
to unlove each other. Instead let's cook
something elaborate and not
invite anyone to share it but eat it
all up very very slowly.

—William Matthews

Instauratio

When the doctor pulled the pin
from my elbow and lowered my arm
beside me I still felt it
trussed in traction above my head.
I'd heard of such things,
the amputee whose missing limb blazes
white till he begs
for its second removal.

As I reached to push my hovering
hand out of my face, I found
my arm still anchored, tethering
me to coarse sheets. This is not
my arm, its shoulder buckled,
its fingers curled like a dry leaf.

For weeks I squeezed rubber balls.
Nurses nagged, Touch your thumb
to your fingers. One night
I cradled and craned my arm
toward a pint of milk on the night-
stand. The carton staggered
and slipped as I tried to steady
it to my mouth,

till at last it flooded my limbs
with its ghostly glow. Then
I glided the precarious container
back as though nothing
had happened. I did this over and
over until the carton was empty.

Dinner with Joni

On rare occasions, I cook dinner,
pick a dependable recipe, shop,
buy wine and set a glorious table.
I like to sip while I chop,
and then another, and if
my husband still hasn't shown
I'll have yet another and turn up
Joni Mitchell so loud
the wok shimmies to her beat.
Then I dim the lights,
so I won't be seen
playing air-guitar, belting
It's coming on Christmas
They're cutting down trees
They're putting up reindeer
And singing songs of joy and peace
Oh I wish I had a river
I could skate away on . . .
Inevitably, my husband walks in
unnoticed, because I'm deafened
by my fans' din. He smiles
at my secret stardom.
Lord, (you) loved me so naughty
Made me weak in the knees
I wish I had a river
I could skate away on.
There is no stopping me now.
Do you want—do you want—do
You want
To dance with me baby
I pour him a glass of wine,
Oh I could drink a case of you, darling
And I would still be on my feet
I would still be on my feet.

Spellbound

It is impossible to keep secrets from metal
Too many feelings reflect in the steel of needles
A tarot card falls from the shuffle
Meridians arch into concentric circles

Too many feelings reflect in the steel of needles
You say I keep my pulse on the side of death
Meridians arch into concentric circles
You are revealed as the King of Wands

I keep my pulse on the side of death
As each needle pierces my skin
You appear as the King of Wands
Crossing the lovers card beneath the queen

Sometimes when a needle pierces my skin
I hold my breath to still the pain
You cross the lovers beneath the queen
I blurt out what I've held back

Holding my breath to still the pain
A gypsy divines, you see what lies beneath
I blurt out what I've held back
Venus spins retrograde in Gemini

You see what lies beneath
So much slips through the eye of a needle
Venus spins retrograde in my sun sign
You point out how reality is an obstacle

So much slips through the eye of a needle
Did you implant the one for clarity
To point out that reality is an obstacle
That I'm confusing longing with love

Did you implant the needle for clarity
So I'd realize that I've rewritten reality
That I confuse longing with love
What seems inevitable may be impossible

I realize I may have rewritten reality
A tarot card falls from the shuffle
Is what seemed unavoidable now attainable
It is impossible to keep secrets from metal

Real Estate

When a house-hunter announced,
If I lived here, I'd chop
those hemlocks down.
They block the view.
I wanted to tell him about
their umbrage at twilight, how
they glow golden in September,
bow like horses
under snow, and fill
our home at Christmas
with their raw scent.
I wanted him to know
that there is one
that draped its branches over me
the night I stood outside and sobbed,
that it still nods when I speak
while the others stand still.
I wanted to tell him that,
especially that.

Our Children's Faces

You probably think
that because not much time
has passed between my husband
and you that all the little things I do
I did with him.

You need to know
that I never laid my head
on his chest and drifted to sleep.
Oh, I tried it once, but my neck ached
and I waited for his steady breath

before I stole to the other side
of the bed like an escaped captive.
I never wanted children,
yet I dream our children's faces
and imagine you and I sneaking

glances, hiding smiles that relish
their earnestness. Know these things
are new to me at the glorious
age of fifty-two.

Again

You're a night-owl,
I tire and rise
with sparrows.
You're athletic,
I crave nothing
more than to stay
in bed with my books
and cats.
When you ask
me to go canoeing
I worry how long
I'll have to be there;
when you suggest
golf, I wonder why
ruin a field. Yet
we listen
each evening
to each other's
work, offer
suggestions
and raise
our glasses
saying,
You did it,
you did it again.

The Adirondacks

Metallic light blurs mountains,
streams, lakes and sky. My body,
a map of rivulets you fold deftly,
scouting hidden waterfalls
that sport such magnitude we both
fear we'll be taken downriver.

Just beyond the terrace, a white pine
rustles its branches like a warning.
You with your constant, elegant gloom
predict the family farm will never sell.
Even if it does, the new owners will level
the house, you say partly to razz me,

then laugh as I roll my eyes on cue.
We sip wine in the alpenglow,
silenced by glacier spills
of granite boulders, the wilderness
of the darkening sky.
It begins to snow.

Torohill

Last night I dreamt I went to Manderly again.
. . . for a while I could not enter, for the way was
barred to me.

—Daphne DuMaurier

Your dead aunt's chimney stands
like a blacksmith's forge as you crest
the drive, your home surrounded
by a cemetery of stone foundations,
tumbling tenant houses and trees old
as fairy tales about to topple. A staircase
rises to the brambled sky. Your grandfather's
mansion turned hotel lies charred
from a jilted piano player
who murdered his lover,
then shot himself in a sea of blinking
ancestors. Ponies decay
in the paddock, while the pool,
tennis courts, and gardens are forgotten
even by deer. Taxes that could choke
a horse. There's Crazy Kate down
in the ruins forever building walls,
flying her blue-blooded flag
like a Keep Out sign, hoarding
matches, storing cans of gasoline.

Zucchinis

What was supposed to be the best summer of my life,
the summer meant for exotic travels and reclining
on chaises eating fried zucchini blossoms was scrapped

when Joni Mitchell sang, You could have been more—
which picked the scab that oozed my mother
and my only trips were on bumper stickers where

I was everyone's redcap, and the drought parched
my vegetable garden, while my husband who did most
of the cooking thought flowers were too beautiful to eat.

Tom's Bands

The Manchilds, The Wormwood Scrubs,
The Counts, Pure Space, The Happy Fish
and Chicken Band, The Manchilds II, Blue
Goose, Quarry Road, Larry and the Shoes,
The Rockabilly Shufflers, Cabin Fever, The
Secrets, Katie and the Meadow Muffins,
Gramolini, Angel Train, The Blue Hill
Kickers, The Sourmash Boys, Somebody's
Sister, Armadillo, Celtic Clan, Sunday's
Well, Inchicore, The Dublin City Ramblers,
The Luck of the Draw, The Urban Legends,
The Unreliable Narrators, Mister Cranky.

Angels of the French Quarter

For Emily

Child angels band together
on the Rue Bourbon
with faces like street urchins,
giggling behind French doors,
turrets and gables.

Gliding from verandas,
they trail behind transvestites,
tug their feathers and snare
their heels in manhole covers.
Splashing Dixie from trumpets and tubas

they swing from ancient oaks
like cherubic apples, their wings
plump as plums.
When you try to photograph them
their faces mist, with their sooty dresses.

In a smoky café behind louvered doors,
they guide us to my grandmother,
Maggie, thirty years in the grave.
Her heavenly hat bops to the beat.
Her round face exalted,

her hair in waves close to her head.
We dance all night, Grandma and I,
wearing wings like Spanish moss
draped from our shoulders.
Feathers flap from our shoes.

At dawn, sleepy dancers tumble
to the cemetery by the river and fade
into the stone of the headless angel
kneeling with a prayer book forever.

They Say Ghosts Can Attach Themselves to Furniture

I. The Music Stand

It's listed as a music stand,
yet its top shelf is steadfast,
unwilling to prop even a nursery round.
It could be dismissed as a dust collector's
paradise—a keeper of knickknacks—
but I'm thinking étagère.
I keep an eye on its mahogany shelves
as you and your siblings divvy
your parents' things. Others tape
their names on end-tables and secretaries.
Apple-pickers run their fingers over
its plump wood, while your family hauls
their histories to storage and Dumpster.

After the estate sale, the music stand waits
in dust-mote radiance. You say,
It's still here because it's ugly, but
this whatnot and I know what it's like
to lose a home held dear.
As I polish its bric-a-brac trim,
I find a drawer tucked in its base.
Is this where your mother hid her journals
until even here was too risky
or where she buried her jewels before
they disappeared? If I uncovered something
priceless, would I turn it in to be counted
or keep the secret
known only by your mother,
the shelves and, now, me?

II. The Piano

Only the trills of scales are heard
through empty rooms. The family
about to buy the farm is still
in their rented house, their boys
scaling the hill out back.

Their father piles documents
in a briefcase for tomorrow's closing.
At the farm, the piano tuner sits
on blue velvet. Finish faded,
you shouldn't have kept it

near the fireplace, but its ivories
are gems and the felt on the hammers!
You decide to keep it.
Your brother is in the driveway hurling
everything left into the Dumpster.

You can't throw books away, you say,
piling cartons on the front porch.
Bemused, you take a white,
porcelain cow head
from the fodder, mounting it

above the dining room fireplace.
The cow's black eyes gleam
as movers dismantle the piano,
discovering legs propped backwards
for decades. The neglected horse

watches the piano movers' white truck
leave the driveway, while the buyers
pack their last carton and put their boys

to bed. It's a miracle this piano never
collapsed. The cow grins, imagining

crushed tots. The piano is transported
to your house where it fits
so miraculously the spell is broken.
The cow curses
the steadfastness of music.

Certain

For Tom

There's no use in stopping.
I will make up for my husband's fallen
life by loving someone else.
I will know him when he sits
at the next table in a restaurant,
or passes me on the road.
I will know what to feed
his injured heart, how to steady
him from slipping, and will finally
be able to ride shotgun
without losing everything.
I will even venture down roads
where tragedies struck—
certain, at last.

Dog Shows and Church

were what we did together.
Only in church Dad preached
from the pulpit as Mom and I
were judged by the congregation.
Not at all like the conformation shows
where I wandered from breed to breed
rolling their names off my tongue:
Bichon Frise,
Rhodesian Ridgeback,
Kuvasz,
Weim—ar—an—er.
Each a perfect union
of syllables rippling across bone.

As my mother and father prayed
for first place, I'd steal
off to a stream and skim Jesus
bugs hoping to find
their water-walking miracles
or climb in the bench stalls
to nap with Grafton
and Blue and Muldoon.
How I loved their soft tongues,
their furrowed brows,
the long leather of their ears.
I knew every Bloodhound
shown in the Northeast.

Best in Show was celebrated
with a cocktail party at a breeder's home.
Oil paintings of champions
lined stairwells like stations of the cross,
while ribbons and silver cups
heralded from curio cabinets.
No one fretted about dogs

sprawled across Oriental rugs,
couches stuffed with goose down,
or the commas of slobber that winged
through the air and anointed us
every time they shook their heads.
This is heaven, I thought.

Jesus of the Brazen and Selfish

Growing up as a priest's daughter
I worked hard at being bad, being anything
but what was expected
and yet when I look back
I did everything I was told.

Unlike my mother who danced
over Celtic swords in the kitchen
and flung mashed potatoes on our plates
so we'd know she wasn't staying.
To get out of her parents' home

she married my father and was disowned
for marrying a bloody Protestant,
then converted to Episcopal,
had an affair, divorced, and married a Jew.
I married the Irish Catholic

of my grandparents' dreams
who raises his pint each evening
with the same square, callused hands,
his ancestors peering from the same mass
hunger graves as mine. Before we met

I knew we'd marry and that the three
girls who stand under the eaves at dusk
would never be born. Only God knows
it's not because I'm unable,
but because I don't want them.

I could never put my pen down
to mash potatoes or drive to Little League,
so I keep those girls in their shadows
where my mother kept me.
When I married, my husband told me

I prayed improperly. He said it's brazen
to speak directly to Jesus. I must kneel
to a saint or the Blessed Virgin
and ask that my prayer be wrapped
in a grape leaf to ponder

when nothing else is pressing.
I told him I've spoken to Jesus
since before I was born when I was
one of those girls hiding between
steamer trunks stamped Ireland.

I told him how Jesus held
his hands out to me when I died,
how without words he asked if I was ready
to remain by his side, how when I answered,
No, he said, Go back.

I told my husband how when I woke
the next morning in the hospital I knew
I'd stayed because I have more
stories like this one to tell,
or maybe it's just that I'm brazen and selfish.

After

No matter what event
we go back for,
you find a reason to drive
by your family's farm.
We've made a pact to hate
the new owners—
the Pig and the Pickerel.
How dare they put their stamp
on your history.
Thank God you took the piano.
I had a theory it would inspire.
You scan the yard—grubby chairs
on the front porch, the tenant horse
still too thin.
I remember the estate sale,
your mother whispering in my ear,
Keep working and stand tall. Sorry,
I'm not making fun of you, Dear,
while you took photos
of every item bought
next to its new owners,
the yard-sale-cult buzzing
mere dollars for your past.
I'm touched that you care
so much, you said.
Stricken, you didn't see
that your melancholy
nostalgia is the place
I want to call home.

Loosestrife

grows rampant in the meadow,
its fuchsia-purple burns
in autumn light.
Don't let it creep
into your garden, people warn,
it'll choke your flowers.
But I want its spiked beauty.
Seedlings sprout through
floorboards, hallways thicken
with tangled discord
till I cannot see
beyond it.

Acknowledgments

Acknowledgments

Grateful acknowledgment is made to the editors of the following journals and anthologies where some of the poems in this book, or earlier versions of them, first appeared.

The Comstock Review "Real Estate"; *Cumberland Poetry Review* "Angels of the French Quarter," "Dorothy at Grasmere," "Everything You Need to Know about Ghosts," "Dinner with Joni," "Sleeping with the Carpenter"; *Hudson Valley Echoes* "Still Life"; *Kalliope* "Plumbing and Psychosis"; *J Journal* "Jesus of the Brazen and Selfish," "Rage," "Torohill"; *The Lullwater Review* "Texas"; *Mudfish* "Night," "Two Rooms Left," "Vicodin"; *The New York Quarterly* "Cowboys"; *Poetry in Performance # 29* "Plumbing and Psychosis," *# 30* "Everything You Need to Know about Ghosts"; *Promethean* "Green Stairs," "Missing Boy"; *Rattle* "Dinner with Joni"; *The Same* "Certain," "They Say Ghosts Attach Themselves to Furniture"; *Snake Nation Review* "Going for Coffee After an Al-Anon Meeting"; *The Yale Journal for Humanities in Medicine* "Instauratio," "Needle's Eye"; *Zone 3* "View from the Playground"

"Certain," "Again," "The Adirondacks," "Torohill," "Tom's Bands," "They Say Ghosts Can Attach Themselves to Furniture," "Evidence," "After," & "No Passing Zone" were included in *Certain*, a chapbook published by Finishing Line Press, 2012. "View from the Playground," "Missing Boy," & "Dog Shows and Church" were included in *Dog Shows and Church, a sequence of poems*, a chapbook published by Eurydice Press, 2000. "Still Life," "Texas," & "View from the Playground" were included in the chapbook *Incantations*, also by Eurydice Press, 1994.

"Still Life" appeared in *Women and Death, 108 American Poets* (Ground Torpedo Press, 1994).
"Dog Shows and Church" appeared in *e, The 1996 Emily Dickinson Award Anthology* (Universities West Press, 1997).
"Everything You Need to Know about Ghosts" appeared in *Chance of a Ghost*, An Anthology of Contemporary Ghost Poems (Helicon Nine Editions, 2005).
"Sempronia" appeared in *Killer Verse, Poems of Murder and Mayhem* (Everyman's Library Pocket Poets, Alfred A. Knopf, 2011.)

This book was a finalist for the Violet Reed Haas Prize for three consecutive years (Snake Nation Press, 2009, 2010, & 2011).

My sincere thanks to The City College of New York for choosing me for The Meyer Cohn Essay Award in Literature in 2001 and The James Ruoff Memorial Essay Award in 2002.

I am grateful to Jeffrey Haste, Meg Kearney, April Ossmann, Steven Huff, Judith Baumel, Estha Weiner, Janet Hamill, Mary Makofske, Donna Spector, Rick Pernod and Stephen Cramer for their encouragement, editorial advice, and generous friendships. And special thanks to my husband, Tom Miller, who always puts whatever he's doing aside to read a first draft, offer suggestions and who has graced many of the poems in this book with his magnificent music.

I am also indebted to Gary Firstenberg, whom I called out of the blue to ask permission to use his beautiful photograph, *Two Old Cars in the Woodstock Forest,* for my cover and he gave it to me, no questions asked. www.firstinphoto.com

Notes and Dedications

The epigraph in "Night" is an inscription Li-Young Lee wrote in his book, *Book of My Nights*, BOA Editions, Ltd., 2001.

"Six Degrees" is for Debbie and Dean Krzymowski.

The epigraph in "Dorothy at Grasmere" is from *Letters of Dorothy Wordsworth* edited by Alan G. Hill, Oxford, 1967.

The epigraph in "Beliefs" is from a song written by Tom Miller called *Where do Storms Go?*

The epigraph in "Vicodin" is a quote from Mary Karr's book, Lit, Harper, 2009.

"Cowboys" is for Marianne Murray and Pam Houston, whose book *Cowboys Are My Weakness*, W.W. Norton & Company, 1980, was an inspiration.

The title "Instauratio" is Latin for rejuvenation and renewal.

The italicized words in "Dinner with Joni" are lyrics written and sung by Joni Mitchell. They are from her songs *River, All I Want,* and *A Case of You,* originally recorded on *Blue,* Reprise Records, 1971.

The epigraph in "Torohill" is from the book *Rebecca,* by Daphne DuMaurier, Avon Books, 1938.

"Angels of the French Quarter" is for Emily Di Tolla.

"Certain" is, of course, for Tom.

ABOUT THE AUTHOR

Donna Reis is the author of the nonfiction book, *Seeking Ghosts in the Warwick Valley* (Schiffer Publishing, Ltd., 2003), and three poetry chapbooks: *Incantations* (Eurydice Press, 1995), *Dog Shows and Church, A Sequence of Poems* (Eurydice Press, 2000) and *Certain* (Finishing Line Press, 2012). She is co-editor and contributor to the anthology, *Blues for Bill: A Tribute to William Matthews* (The University of Akron Press, 2005). Her poems have appeared in numerous other anthologies and journals including *Beyond Lament: Poets of the World Bearing Witness to the Holocaust* (Northwestern University Press, 1998), *Chance of a Ghost* (Helicon Nine Editions, 2005) and *Killer Verse: Poems of Murder and Mayhem* (Everyman's Library, Alfred A. Knopf 2011). She received her Master of Arts Degree in Creative Writing from The City College, City University of New York, in 2002.

She is an avid quilter and teaches poetry at The Northeast Poetry Center, College of Poetry in Warwick, New York. She and her husband, writer and musician Tom Miller, live in New York's Hudson River Valley. They are working on a recording of music and poetry.